Daughters Arise!: Possess Your Power

ISBN: 0-9744178-1-5

Daughters Arise!:

Possess Your Power

Dr. Fred Henley

www.daughtersarise.com

Daughters Arise!:
Possess Your Power

CONTENTS

This Book Is Dedicated To My Late Mother For Giving Me The Gift And Love Of Learning; To My Wife Who Gives Me The Love And Security To Follow My Dreams; To My Grandmother Who Gave Me The Gift Of Simple Faith And Prayer; To My Aunt For Believing With Me And To My Pastor For Giving Me A Living Example For Daughters Arise. Finally, To All Of The Women That God Has Used To Feed And Nurture My Growth And Development

STATEMENT OF PURPOSE

THIS BOOK IS WRITTEN FOR MY DAUGHTERS, TAYLER & CHRISTIAN AND DAUGHTERS THROUGH-OUT THE WORLD THAT THEY WOULD BE EN-LIGHTENED, EMPOWERED AND ENCOURAGED BY THE WORDS FOUND WITHIN THESE PAGES.

INTRODUCTION

My dearest daughters,

This book is written from the deepest depths of my love and concern for you and your ability to succeed in a world that is weighted against you from the moment that you draw your first breath of life until the moment that you take your last breath. My love for the two of you and all of the other daughters born in this generation throughout the world led me to the inescapable conclusion that a manual for success was needed to navigate this journey of life as a daughter.

I will share with you my success and my scars. I will share my joy and my pain as well as my highs and my lows.

NO ONE CAN MAKE YOU FEEL INFERIOR WITH-
OUT YOUR CONSENT

ELEANOR ROOSEVELT

It would be easy, but not helpful, to speak from a detached, clinical perspective and not expose my flaws and our family's failures. You need to see the scars in order to avoid the same ones. You need to see the stars, so that you can become one.

In the tradition of our ancestors, I will tell you how we got over. A deep, abiding faith in God delivered our ancestors from slavery and a multitude of other horrors. My search for such biblical wisdom led me to an obscure group of women in the Old Testament. The Daughters of Zelophehad first appear in the wilderness demanding a portion of their father's inheritance.

THINK WRONGLY, IF YOU PLEASE, BUT IN ALL
CASES THINK FOR YOURSELF

DORIS LESSING

Over three thousand years ago, five sisters with strange names challenge the existing legal system and prevailing status quo of their day and win. We will begin our journey at a point prior to their father, Zelophehad's death and immediately following the death of my mother at the young age of 35.

In a perfect world, this book would not have to be written or read. In a perfect world, all persons would be treated equally in terms of opportunities to maximize their individual potential. In a perfect world, daughters would be afforded the same respect and access that sons take for granted.

This book is therefore written to enlighten and inspire the hearts and minds of daughters. All females are daughters.

DON'T COMPROMISE YOURSELF. YOU ARE ALL YOU'VE
GOT.

JANIS JOPLIN

This book is written for all individuals born of the female gender. It is written for daughters rather than females or women because the word "daughter" carries with the implicit recognition of an underlying biological relationship with other humans called parents.

The full complexity of the parent-child relationship and all of its nuances is well beyond the scope of this slim volume, but suffice it to say that daughters are unique. The care and nurture of daughters is unique due to a host of familial and societal issues that are likewise beyond the scope of this volume.

This book however will focus its attention on the impact of a father's wisdom, counsel and encouragement on the success of daughters

WHEN HIT, HIT BACK

AUTHOR

by examining the success of the Daughters of Zelophehad and their father's impartation of confidence, strength and boldness into their lives.

In the same way that we can look to collapsed buildings and observe that there was an earthquake in the area or see trees uprooted and homes blown apart by wind and conclude that there was a hurricane or tornado in the area, we can often look to successful and powerful women and find a dynamic and enriching relationship with a father. Unfortunately, this is not the reality for all daughters due to a natural father's inability or neglect of responsibility.

For daughters that have not known or experienced a positive relationship with their natural father, may Daughters Arise! impart wisdom, encouragement and strength for your journey. For daughters that have known and experienced a positive relationship with their fathers, may Daughters Arise! remind you of and supplement the love, support and encouragement of your natural father. Most importantly, may Daughters Arise! remind all daughters that your Father in heaven loves you and wills the best for your lives.

LESSON 1

Life isn't fair

The hammer shatters glass, but it forges steel
Russian Proverb

On October 29, 1976, my twelfth birthday, I sat in the front row of St. Mary's Catholic Church as my mother was eulogized. As I sat through the Delta Sigma Theta Omega Service that I did not understand, I heard my mother's sorority sisters speak kind words about her. I did not realize that during those moments of numbness that I was going through a transition.

You don't think about transitions at the age of 12, but later in life I often looked back to October 25, 1976, the day when my

DR. FRED HENLEY

PAIN FREQUENTLY PROCEEDS PROGRESS

AUTHOR

world was shattered. October 25, 1976 was the day that my father told my sister and I that my mother had been killed in a single car accident.

I have lived this first lesson for more than twenty five (25) years. The most fundamental of all lessons for possessing your power is that life is not fair. Tragedy of all sorts strike homes of every hue and complexion. Easy answers to the question of why are never found, nevertheless we accept our plight and move on in spite of it. I have often looked back to overcome obstacles, challenges and setbacks. It is important to embrace affliction because it will allow you to spring into your future.

As reflected in our opening proverb, we can be both crushed

DR. FRED HENLEY

I THINK MYSELF HAPPY
ACTS 26:1

and molded by the same tool. Thus, always remember that your response to life's unfairness will determine whether you are crushed or molded by your circumstances. Paul, the apostle, shares another great principle to couple with the acceptance that life is not fair. Paul's principle is that we can respond to life's unfairness by choosing to be happy despite the unfairness.

Paul's statement "I think myself happy" was made while on trial for his life in Rome. This concept has been called the power of positive thinking by Dr. Norman Vincent Peale or positive mental attitude by other great success experts such as W. Clement Stone and Napoleon Hill. Please be clear that life will bring a certain amount of pain and discomfort that you can not magically think away.

SUCCESS IS TO BE MEASURED NOT SO MUCH BY
THE POSITION THAT ONE HAS REACHED IN LIFE
AS BY THE OBSTACLES THAT ONE HAS OVERCOME
WHILE TRYING TO SUCCEED

BOOKER T. WASHINGTON

You can not think away tragedy, but can choose how you will think in response to tragedy. Choose to think happy thoughts in sad situations and you will be amazed that your life will follow the direction of your thoughts. Although I had no choice in my mother's death and quite honestly still bear a portion of that pain, I have to choose on a daily basis to be either a bitter or a better person.

We can look to our biblical text found in the 27th chapter of the book of Numbers to see how Zelophehad addressed the unfairness of life. We must assume that at some point prior to his death, Zelophehad gathered his five daughters and told them that his own issues in the wilderness would keep him

DR. FRED HENLEY

YOU CAN CHOOSE
TO BE BITTER OR BETTER,
BUT NOT BOTH.

AUTHOR

from acquiring his piece of the Promised Land.

Zelophehad explained to his daughters that the laws of inheritance would prevent his piece of the Promised Land from passing to his children because he had no sons. Zelophehad told them that his name meant first born which in his time entitled him to certain advantages and preferences over and above his other siblings. Thus, he was clear on the protocol of the day as it related to the inheritance rights of daughters.

It can be assumed that he had five daughters in an effort to father a son who would care for his mother and sisters. After five attempts, Zelophehad had to accept the fact that he would be the father of five

DR. FRED HENLEY

THINGS DON'T CHANGE. YOU CHANGE YOUR WAY
OF LOOKING, THAT'S ALL

CARLOS CASTANEDA

daughters. Sensing the extreme injustice and unfairness of the inheritance laws, Zelophehad vowed that his inability to receive his inheritance would not prevent him from leaving a legacy to his daughters.

Zelophehad knew that you are not living until you are giving. Likewise, he knew that a person is judged by the response to a mistake not the fact that a mistake has been made. Thus, notwithstanding his own failure, Zelophehad's response was to raise daughters that would change the legal system.

As reflected at the outset of this journey, this is not a perfect world. Although daughters make up half of the world's population, they control very little of the world's resources, governments or corporations. In

DR. FRED HENLEY

YOU CAN'T BE BRAVE IF YOU'VE ONLY HAD WON-
DERFUL THINGS HAPPEN TO YOU

MARY TYLER MOORE

fact, as of this writing in 2002, only six corporations listed on the Fortune 500 list of America's largest corporations are controlled by a female Chief Executive Officer.

Despite the unfairness of life's circumstances and the inequity in the distribution of wealth and other resources, please understand my daughters that you will find life's greatest challenge facing you in the mirror every morning. The remaining lessons found here will provide you with the blueprint for successfully possessing the power given to you at creation.

Please be clear that as a female you were not created as a second class citizen. While you are endowed with the power of heaven for a function that is

DR. FRED HENLEY

IT'S NEVER TOO LATE, IN FICTION OR IN LIFE, TO
REVISE

NANCY THAYER

unique to your gender, you are also endowed with an equal share of dominion with man. In fact, the elimination of pubic power is necessary to continued evolution of our society, economy and world. Daughters you must arise to positively affect our world. Therefore, please continue on this journey to possessing your power.

DR. FRED HENLEY

MEN AND WOMEN ARE EQUAL IN DOMINION, BUT DIFFERENT IN FUNC-TION

AUTHOR

LESSON 2

Make a Move

"The daughters of Zelophehad....*approached* the entrance to the Tent of Meeting...." Num 27:1-2

The person who moves a mountain begins by carrying away small stones

A journey of a thousand miles must begin with a single step
Chinese Proverbs

Once you have mastered lesson I—"life is not fair", you are ready to walk in the footsteps of the Daughters of Zelophehad. As our opening proverbs reflect, a journey has not begun until the first step is taken and a mountain has not been moved until the first stone is removed. The biblical record states that "the daughters *approached* the tent of meeting" (emphasis supplied).

This was a major undertaking in the society and culture of 3500 years ago. At this time in history, only certain male individuals were allowed to interact with the leadership of Israel and inherit property. Zelophehad's daughters did not work within the chain of command. They ignored it!

In August 1982, I made a move that changed my life. With my father temporarily unavailable due to his own legal issues at the time and my mother residing in heaven, I went to the U-Haul truck center and purchased a one way rental to New Orleans, Louisiana. At 17 years old, I left Port Arthur, Texas to attend Xavier University

DR. FRED HENLEY

FEEL THE FEAR, AND DO IT ANYWAY

SUSAN JEFFERS

in New Orleans, Louisiana without any visible means of support or guarantees of success. With my father's legal affairs a part of my small hometown's general conversation, I had to overcome the expectation of reaching the same destination as my father.

I was forced to see beyond the obvious limitations placed on a young man with no support and a negative prophecy hovering over his head. The only choice that I had was to ignore the rules that dictated my failure based upon my dysfunctional family history.

In the same way, the Daughters of Zelophehad ignored the fact that no one especially women showed up at the Tent of Meeting unannounced and uninvited.

DR. FRED HENLEY

WE ARE THE CHOICES WE MAKE

MERYL STREEP

DAUGHTERS ARISE!: POSSESS YOUR POWER

You will have to do the same thing in life. There are rules that dictate a marginal existence in certain aspects of your life due to your gender. Although these gender based rules of life should not exist, the truth of the matter is that gender based rules are alive and thriving in our society. Thus, it is necessary to ignore existing boundaries to explore new frontiers.

A modern example of ignoring existing boundaries is Katherine Drexel, who has been canonized as a saint by the Roman Catholic Church. As a young woman born into the wealthy Drexel family, Katherine Drexel possessed immense wealth and a heart for the poor and downtrodden particularly Indians and African Americans. When she contacted the Pope to request that something be done to

DR. FRED HENLEY

IGNORE EXISTING BOUNDARIES TO EXPLORE
NEW FRONTIERS.

AUTHOR

assist the Indian and African American people, the Pope challenged Katherine to use her wealth and ability to make a difference.

Katherine Drexel had to make a move. She had to either put up or shut up. Katherine Drexel made her move and founded a school in New Orleans that she named Xavier Preparatory. Xavier Preparatory gave birth to Xavier University, which is now the leading producer of African American medical students in the entire United States. As a student at Xavier University, I learned that the Latin phrase on the school seal meant, "With God as our helper, we have nothing to fear".

Since Katherine Drexel started her educational outreach at a time when women did not

SEIZE THE DAY, PUT NO TRUST IN TOMORROW

HORACE

have the right to vote, it can safely be assumed that she relied on God as her help each and every step of the way. In many ways, we are often limited by our own inability to see new possibilities because we are so often influenced by what we have seen in the past.

President Franklin Delano Roosevelt, whose domestic policies helped to rescue America from the Great Depression, put it best when he said "above all, try something". Don't be afraid to risk what you have in order to gain what you don't have. In most instances, what you have does not measure up to what you could have if you were only willing to take a risk.

Never allow the security of today imprison the promise of tomorrow. Your life is a gift from God to you and the use of your life is your gift to God and others. When in doubt about making a move, remember the words of the great entrepreneur and founder of the Mary Kay cosmetics company, Mary Kay Ash who said, "if you think you can, you can. And if you think you can't, you are right".

Finally, use the strength and wisdom of the ages that has emboldened women for centuries to do more, see more and be more. Use the wisdom that acknowledges that your life and existence is a special gift from God Almighty to your generation and the generations that will follow you. Please make a move for the world. Your generations are depending on you.

DR. FRED HENLEY

**NEVER ALLOW THE SECURITY OF TODAY TO IM-
PRISON THE PROMISE OF TOMORROW**

AUTHOR

LESSON THREE

Take a Stand

"The daughters of Zelophehad …approached the entrance to the Tent of Meeting and *stood* before Moses, Eleazar the priest, the leaders and the whole assembly…." Num 27:1-3

My only concern was to get home after a hard day's work
Rosa Parks

After making a move, it is absolutely necessary to take a stand for your dream to come true. While making a move requires boldness, taking a stand requires courage. Boldness plus courage equal power. Boldness will cause you to pursue your own dream, but courage will allow you to stand when others oppose it. Always remember there is no greater power in this world than the possession of your own dream. The fulfillment of your dream will certainly require divine assistance to become reality, but the first step is for you to own your dream.

Zelophehad certainly warned his daughters that courage was absolutely necessary to face the authority figures that established the rules for a male dominated society. The Daughters of Zelophehad had to show up at the Tent of Meeting. A place that was unfamiliar to them and a place that women were unwelcome.

Once they arrived at the Tent of Meeting, the Daughters of Zelophehad had to stand before Moses and the Elders of Israel and make their case for receiving their father's inheritance. After

DR. FRED HENLEY

BOLDNESS PLUS COURAGE EQUALS POWER

AUTHOR

making their case, they had to stand and await a decision from Almighty God.

You will find yourselves in similar situations throughout your life. You will have to stand before those in authority and make your case for equal participation in the distribution of wealth and power. History is full of wonderful examples of women that took a stand and changed the world.

Rosa Parks refused to give up a seat on a bus in Montgomery, Alabama and the modern civil rights movement in the United States was born. Mrs. Parks said she was only trying to get home, but her bold stand for what was right, moral and just ignited a movement that continues today nearly fifty years later.

DR. FRED HENLEY

LIFE IS OURS TO BE SPENT, NOT TO BE SAVED

D.H. LAWRENCE

Taking a personal stand will require you to believe in yourself despite what the world or others thinks about you. My life would have ended in a small town in Texas if I had listened to the naysayers who told me that my life would not amount to anything. I had to take a stand and believe in myself to arise out of my position and condition. It is vitally important that you look beyond all of the obvious sources for help and look instead for unlikely alliances that have been preordained by God.

One of my preordained alliances was with a high school counselor. Ms. Arreader P. Guidry was my counselor at Lincoln High School and she wanted to help me despite my family history because she had helped my mother during her educational career. One of the reasons that this book is being written is to pour out some of the goodness that has been poured into me by Ms. Guidry and others that have helped me throughout my life. Take your stand and accept help from those sent to help you and you will possess your power.

Seek strength within and take a stand. Victory will be yours in the end.
Miep Gies

LESSON FOUR

Make a Demand

"The daughters of Zelophehad ...said...[g]ive us property among our father's relatives." Num 27:

It's better to be a lion for a day than a sheep all your life
Sister Elizabeth Kenny

After instructing his daughters on the need to make a move and to take a stand, Zelophehad spoke to them about the most important, but also the most dangerous, step to possessing their inheritance and consequently their power in the Promised Land. The most important step to possessing your power is to make a demand. It is interesting, however, that the demand must be made first on your own ability, courage and talents.

If your book is not written, your business is not started or your attempt at greatness is not made, a crime has been committed. The world has been robbed of joy that is found only within the wealth of your special ability.

A fundamental premise of such a philosophy is that God created only one of you and hence designed you to do something that only you can do. The world discourages individual difference, but celebrates individual genius. In many instances, genius is wasted by those afraid to step out and be different.

After you have made a demand on your own ability, you are prepared to make a demand

**DREAM BIG
BELIEVE BIG
TALK BIG
LIVE BIG**

AUTHOR

on those people or systems that stand between you and the fulfillment of your potential. In the case of the Daughters of Zelophehad, they had to not only face Moses and the authority figures of
their day, but also centuries of gender prejudiced tradition that
subjugated women to subservient, meaningless roles in society.

Zelophehad's training to make a demand is most evident in
his daughters' simple, but powerful request. The Daughters sim-
ply said, "give us property". This unequivocal demand should be
noted for its boldness in light of times in which they lived. It has
been forbidden, unthinkable, even considered insane for a woman
to demand anything over the entire course of human history.

DR. FRED HENLEY

**ASK FOR MORE THAN YOU EXPECT TO RECEIVE,
DON'T BE SURPRISED WHEN YOU GET IT**

AUTHOR

Over 3500 years ago, the Daughters of Zelophehad's demand for property made an indelible mark on the history of women's rights. This monumental occasion in history is significant because it ignored all the inherent obstacles to making the initial demand. It is most significant because the Daughters of Zelophehad demanded property which carried with it stature, position and authority.

As a property owner in ancient times, you possessed the right to govern your land and speak out on issues affecting the community at large. By demanding and receiving property, the Daughters of Zelophehad guaranteed themselves a seat at the table of power.

A simple lesson to be acquired from this incident in ancient history is that your demand should be simple, direct and meaningful. Your demand should not require complicated explanations from experts. The demand should not require consultation with multiple parties for a decision. Finally, the demand should seek to possess something that will make a difference in your life.

A wonderful example of this principle of a simple, direct and meaningful demand is the women's suffrage movement that guaranteed women the right to vote. It is difficult to believe that women have had the right to vote in the United States for less than 100 years.

DR. FRED HENLEY

AN EFFECTIVE DEMAND IS SIMPLE, DIRECT & MEANINGFUL

AUTHOR

Although Susan B. Anthony and Elizabeth Cady Stanton died before the Amendment to the Constitution that allowed women to vote was finally passed, the demand for the right to vote passed all three tests for an effective demand.

It was simple, direct and meaningful. Susan B. Anthony made a demand for women to vote and today women across America hold many powerful elected positions including Mayor Shirley Franklin of Atlanta and Rep. Nancy Pelosi (D-San Francisco), the Minority Leader of the United States House of Representatives. Some 3500 years ago, daughters did not enjoy the same inheritance rights as sons.

Some 80 years ago, women in the United States were unable

FAILURE IS IMPOSSIBLE

SUSAN B. ANTHONY

to vote. Unfair? No question about it. What was the proper response to this fundamental unfairness? Acquire the power necessary to change the system. Zelophehad undoubtedly told his daughters that power concedes nothing without a demand. While it is utterly important to make a move and to take a stand, you have gained nothing until you make a demand.

There was a point in my life where I decided to get the most out of my God given ability. I made a demand on the natural gifts and talents that were placed within me at birth. There is an interesting lesson to be learned during the process of making a demand on your personal talent and ability. The lesson is that the only resistance that will be encountered is internal.

In other words, you are your own worst enemy when making a personal demand. Ignore the voices of doubt and fear that lurk in the shadows of your mind and shock yourself with the riches that lay just beneath the surface of your doubt and fear. There is a story about an Oklahoma family that worked diligently at farming a large plot of land, but found no success.

They sold the land and moved farther west in search of their wealth and success. The new owner of the farm went out one day and found that the farm was not a farm, but an oilfield. The moral of story is that the riches that you seek are right beneath the surface in your own backyard.

The founder of Bethune Cookman College in Daytona, Florida started her college with less than two dollars and a dream. Almost 100 years later, Mary McLeod Bethune's dream is alive and thriving. She believed her race was not an obstacle to God's ability to meet her hard work and perseverance with favor and grace.

Ms. Bethune's hard work and God's grace elevated her to prominent positions in national politics. She served as an adviser to President Franklin D. Roosevelt and was a good friend of Eleanor Roosevelt, the President's wife. Always remember to demand and to get the most out of your individual ability.

Many of the world's greatest achievements were

WHAT WOULD YOU ATTMEPT TO DO IF YOU
KNEW YOU COULD NOT FAIL?

ROBERT SCHULLER

accomplished after everyone said they were impossible. Bishop Milton Wright said that there was nothing else that could be accomplished by man and that man would never fly. The only problem with Bishop Wright's pronouncements was that his sons, the Wright Brothers flew the first aircraft at Kitty Hawk not long after their father declared flying an impossibility.

The four-minute mile and the conquest of Mount Everest were likewise deemed impossible before Roger Bannister ran right through the world's stopwatch based limitation and Sir Edmund Hilary conquered Mount Everest. The previously impossible has been accompished numerous times since the imaginary barriers were broken by Bannister and Hilary. In fact, many high school athletes today run a mile in less than four minutes.

In sum, your achievements are only limited by your beliefs. Please do not allow the world's limitations to serve as your own boundaries. Use the world's limitations as targets to surpass rather than excuses for mediocre dreams and low aspirations.

.

FORGET TO QUIT
AUTHOR

LESSON FIVE

Know Your History

The daughters of Zelophehad son of Hepher, the son of Gilead, the son of Makir, the son of Manasseh, belonged to the clans of Manasseh son of Joseph. Our father died in the desert. He was not among Korah's followers, who banded together against the LORD, but he died for his own sin and left no sons.
Num 27:

> *Those who cannot remember the past are condemned to repeat it.*
> *George Santayana*

This is the best and most personal part of the book because this lesson will allow you to see the past and use it to influence your future. It is important to know what has happened in the past because knowledge of your history allows you to build on the success and avoid the failure found there. When you visit your physician, she will take a family history of illness to determine an appropriate course of action. In similar fashion, you can take a family inventory and determine what gifts and talents are resident in your family.

There are gifts in every family and there is a gift in You! It is your duty, task & mission to discover it and then develop it for the good of others. When you become aware of the accomplishments of the past, you will become confident in your ability to compete and succeed as well.

DR. FRED HENLEY

NO SINGLE PART OF YOUR PAST IS GREATER
THAN THE SUM TOTAL OF YOUR FUTURE

AUTHOR

Family history is often obscured by personal agendas, shame and missing links to certain parts of the family due to absentee fathers and sometimes disgruntled mothers. Nevertheless, the discovery of your gifts should never be held hostage by ignorance of your history. You must ignore hostility and family secrecy to find the treasure buried in your past.

Zelophehad reminded his daughters of their rich history in order to encourage them to make a history after his death. The Daughters of Zelophehad came from good stock and were predisposed to possessing their power because of their heritage. The Daughters of Zelophehad were from the tribe of Manasseh. Manasseh was one of the two sons born to Joseph during his

**THERE IS A GIFT IN YOU! IT IS YOUR DUTY, TASK
& MISSION TO DISCOVER IT AND THEN DEVELOP
IT FOR THE GOOD OF OTHERS.**

AUTHOR

stay in Egypt. Five generations removed, Joseph was the grand-father of the Daughters of Zelophehad. Joseph's story was certainly an inspiration to the Daughters of Zelophehad. Joseph's story is inspiring to anyone facing trouble and adversity. Joseph was sold into Egyptian slavery by his jealous brothers, but ended up as second in command to Pharoah. While in Egypt, Joseph fathered a son that he named Manasseh which means to forget. Joseph, the ultimate overcomer, knew that forgetting trouble was necessary to moving into the future.

Since the Daughters of Zelophehad knew that forgetting their trouble was mandatory for moving into their future, they were not hindered by their father's mistakes in the wilderness. In fact, the

DR. FRED HENLEY

YOUR PAST IS THE SCHOOLMASTER OF YOUR FUTURE

AUTHOR

Daughters let Moses know that their father died for his own sin in the wilderness. The most important thing was that the Daughters knew enough about their father's issue in the wilderness to know that his issue did not disqualify them from receiving their share of his inheritance.

While we must forget the problems of the past, knowledge of our history is vital because it will allow us to build on the success and avoid the mistakes. Zelophehad knew that it was vitally important to be transparent with his daughters. As a father, I would prefer not to tell you that I have failed financially, professionally, personally, relationally and socially, but I believe that our generations have been plagued by our lack of transparency and honesty.

Honesty and candor is painful, but also liberating. Family secrets allow the enemy of our future success and prosperity to hold our generations in bondage. Pride is the most common reason for maintaining family secrets. All families are concerned about holding on to the family's good name at the expense of the family's future good fortune. Many family problems are generational in nature which means the same problem has affected several generations of the same family.

For instance, a grandfather, father and son all struggle with drinking or gambling. A grandmother, mother and daughter all struggle with anger or depression. If Zelophehad's

YOUR LIFE AS WELL AS YOUR PAST HAS A PURPOSE

AUTHOR

example is followed; we will share the dirty laundry that brings personal embarrassment to the family. Our dirty laundry will expose our family's common enemy and prepare us for victory.

There are many issues and individuals that demonstrate the truth of this point within our family line, but it would not be appropriate to discuss their personal affairs here in this book without their consent and agreement. It is sufficient to note that in this Internet age that there are no more secrets. A click of the mouse will bring up all of your success as well as your failures.

On a recent flight, I sat in my seat listening to the preflight warnings and one of the warnings struck me as relevant

DR. FRED HENLEY

YOUR CLOSEST EXIT MAY BE BEHIND YOU

AUTHOR

to the message of this book.

Having started to travel via aircraft at the age of four or five, I heard the familiar warning in a new and different way. The warning was that in the event of an emergency that the closest exit from the aircraft may be behind the seat in which I was sitting.

This simple statement is vitally important for airline passengers and for daughters seeking to possess their power. The closest exit from your present predicament may be found in your family history. Finding solutions to present problems in past situations requires the willingness to ask tough questions of family members who are often not willing to share their personal embarrassment for your personal

DR. FRED HENLEY

**KNOW WHO YOU ARE AND YOU WILL ENJOY
WHAT YOU HAVE**

AUTHOR

freedom. The reason for this unwillingness to share personal challenges is due to ignorance as to the ways of God.

God often turns the greatest mistakes into the greatest triumphs. The life of King David provides a vivid example of this principle. While David was guilty of adultery with Bathsheba and the murder of her husband, God allowed David and Bathsheba to give birth to Solomon. The book of Matthew records that "David begot Solomon by the one who was Uriah's wife." The mistake is recorded in the bible to remind us that God uses mistakes to change not destroy our lives.

Solomon's contributions to the world include several biblical books of wisdom including Proverbs and Ecclesiastes. Solomon is known as one of the greatest kings in Israel's history in terms of wealth and wisdom.

Therefore David's failure produced a great success in the form of a son that was a great king. An interesting note is that David gave Solomon compelling spiritual advice, but did not address his own failure in his relationships with women. Thus, it is not a surprise that the downfall of Solomon's magnificent kingdom was marriage to many foreign women that did not share his beliefs and values.

In sum, always remember that it is not how you start the race, but how you finish it that counts. God does not judge based on how many times you fall, but how many times that

OUR GREATEST GLORY IS NOT IN NEVER FALL-
ING, BUT IN RISING EVERY TIME WE FALL

CONFUCIUS

you get up to run again. There are several examples within our immediate family that bear this principle out. My mother taught my grandmother to read in her fifties and she is still reading her bible everyday in her nineties. My aunt returned to college in her late fifties and received both her Bachelors and Masters degrees past the age of sixty.

My sixty eight year old father continues to press forward in the pursuit of new goals despite having succeeded and failed in numerous businesses over the last forty years. While short memory of failure is required equipment for the journey to success and significance, it is absolutely vital that you know your family history to maximize and exploit all of the gifts and talents that lie within you.

LESSON SIX

CLEAR & EXPAND

"But Joshua said to the house of Joseph-to Ephraim and Manasseh-"You are numerous and powerful. You will have not only one allotment but the forested hill country as well. *Clear it*, and its farthest limits will be yours; though the Canaanites have iron chariots and though they are strong, *you can drive them out.*" Joshua 17:17-18 (italics added)

In order to arise and possess your power, you must accept as a given that you are going to be disappointed, lied to, cheated on, talked about and mistreated. Your response to these abuses determines how fast and how far you go in life. It is useful to separate and categorize obstacles in the process of overcoming them. Some of our obstacles are purely personal.

It is likely that the majority of our obstacles are personal. There are other obstacles imposed by society and culture on women that must be overcome. History is full of examples of women overcoming societal and cultural barriers.

When you have acquired an understanding of what has been written above, you will still have work to do. For an excellent example, we can look at what happened when the Daughters of Zelophehad arrived in the Promised Land. The land was distributed by tribes of people. The Daughters of Zelophehad belonged to the house of Manasseh.

DR. FRED HENLEY

WHAT DOES NOT DESTROY ME, MAKES ME
STRONG

NIETZSCHE

The land apportioned to the house of Manasseh was large, hilly and tree covered. After receiving the land, the tribes complained to Joshua that they would be unable to live on the land because it was too small and there were enemies in the land.

Joshua immediately spoke to their potential when he told them that they were numerous and powerful. Joshua told them that they would have to clear the land of the trees and enemies in order to possess the full extent of the land. This exchange between Joshua and the Daughters of Zelophehad is a parallel to the dilemma faced everyday by daughters of today.

The opportunities that exist today are available to everyone, but daughters often have to draw on their inner strength to clear the obstacles that block access to opportunity and success. As Joshua stated, daughters must realize that there is strength in numbers. If all the daughters of the United States decided to demanded representation in the White House, a female President could be elected.

There are a number of obstacles that stand in the way of opportunity and success for daughters, but we will only focus on several personal obstacles in order to provide encouragement and hope to daughters. Fear is a major personal obstacle for daughters that must be destroyed. Most fear is born out of a lack of security.

Lack of security is prevalent in fatherless homes. Thus, when the father is absent and uninvolved in a daughter's life, the daughter is less likely to take any chances or demand her right to success.

While the solution to this dilemma requires another book, it is sufficient to note that God is father to the fatherless and the defender of widows. The absence or presence of a natural father is not determinative of your potential for success. A father's presence is vital and important, but a father's absence is not fatal. Your primary responsibility is to get the most out of your ability whether your biological father is involved in your life at this moment.

The fatherless home is often a source of other personal obstacles such as unresolved anger. Unresolved anger over the absence of a father corrodes your own effectiveness.

DR. FRED HENLEY

IF OPPORTUNITY DOESN'T KNOCK, BUILD A DOOR

MILTON BERLE

Bitterness and rage are obstacles that are byproducts of unresolved anger. Let go of your false beliefs about yourself and others. Release the issues that have plagued generations of your family. In order to release the issues of your past, you must first acknowledge that mistakes were made by imperfect people that happen to be related to you.

Perfection is the standard that we use to judge others. When we expect perfection from others, we will always be disappointed. Many families refuse to acknowledge the problems of the past and consequently remain imprisoned by the secrets buried within the family bloodline. The price of freedom from family secrets is discomfort. When we face our family secrets, we are forced into the uncomfortable position of confronting our loved ones.

If we refuse to confront when it is necessary to clear the obstacles in our path, we will find ourselves living out our lives in bondage to past hurts. An example for this principle is found in the life of Gideon. In biblical times, Gideon's father was an idol worshipper. This created a dilemma for Gideon. He was a member of the tribe of Manasseh and therefore a relative of the Daughters of Zelophehad.

Gideon saw himself as weak and worthless due to his family name and tribal membership. When the Angel of the Lord visited Gideon, the first task given to him was to destroy his father's idols. He was so afraid to destroy the idols that he carried out the task at

DR. FRED HENLEY

**IT IS BETTER TO LIGHT ONE CANDLE THAN TO
CURSE THE DARKNESS**

CHRISTOPER SOCIETY, MOTTO

night. He went on to become a fearless leader of Israel's army during his lifetime. The principle here is that you will never see the future until you destroy the bondage of your past.

DR. FRED HENLEY

WITH GOD AS OUR HELPER, WE HAVE NOTHING
TO FEAR

XAVIER UNIVERSITY OF LOUISIANA, MOTTO

LESSON SEVEN

ACCEPT ADVERSITY

The way I see it, if you want the rainbow, you gotta put up with the
rain

Dolly Parton

Although you have learned that life is not fair. It is necessary to note that more is required for possessing your power. You must not only know that life is not fair, but you must also accept adversity as part of the process for possessing your power. The Daughters of Zelophehad knew that their bold actions were subject to controversy and adversity. Zelophehad certainly warned his daughters that adversity was a required element in achieving the goal of gaining their inheritance.

As shown below, the willingness to accept adversity was an inherited family trait for the Daughters of Zelophehad. The Daughters were members of the tribe of Manasseh. Manasseh was one of the sons born to Joseph during his time in Egypt.

Joseph was one of the sons of Jacob. Joseph was the equivalent of a Prime Minister of Egypt and was second in command in leadership of the country. Joseph answered only to Pharaoh in terms of his authority. If the story of Joseph started and ended with him sitting next to Pharaoh, it would be a wonderful example of starting and staying on top of the heap.

FOCUS ON WHAT'S LEFT NOT WHAT 'S LOST

AUTHOR

Joseph's story illustrates a much more accurate picture of life. From Joseph's story, there are vital principles for accepting adversity and ultimately possessing your power. Joseph's ultimate attitude was that he would not assume that the person or persons behind his misfortune were in control of his present circumstances or his future condition.

Accepting adversity requires a change in perspective. In order to develop this change in perspective, Joseph's story provides several powerful life lessons. First, know who is in charge. Joseph endured several years of slavery and imprisonment in a foreign land, but he never lost sight of the fact that God was and still is in control.

AFFLICTION BRINGS TRANSITION TO GREATER PURPOSE

AUTHOR

The Daughters of Zelophehad were unfairly stripped of their inheritance, but they knew that God was in charge. Likewise, it is necessary for you to see that despite your obstacles God is in charge.

On the other side of a bad day is a day of limitless opportunities. When we choose to see grasshoppers rather than grapes, our lives are nothing more than a race to death rather than an all out sprint to use every minute of every hour to extract every ounce of life that exists in the 24 hour segment of time that we call today.

It is only when we embrace disadvantages and misfortune that we can fully examine and appreciate the issues and opportunities that our finite existence provides in this

DR. FRED HENLEY

YOU MAY BE DISAPPOINTED IF YOU FAIL, BUT
YOU ARE DOOMED IF YOU DON'T TRY

BEVERLY SILLS

lifetime. Likewise, lives that are not stretched into discomfort will not develop into all that God has ordained.

There is a point when you recognize that you can have anything that you can create in your mind. For example, this book existed in my mind well before it ever appeared in bookstores or on the internet. When you have cleared your personal obstacles, there are no boundaries to what can be achieved through concentrated effort and focus on your goals. The point here is that your dreams should not be limited by your obstacles.

ALL THINGS WORK TOGETHER FOR THE GOOD

ROMANS 8:28

CONCLUSION

There is no need to repeat the lessons provided above. The book is intentionally brief in order to allow you to read and re-read and digest the information given here under the inspiration of Almighty God. It is my hope that the words here enlighten, empower and encourage you to reach out and grab the power given to you by your heavenly Father. In the words of Jesus to Jairus' dead daughter, I say unto you

DAUGHTERS ARISE! ARISE! ARISE!

ABOUT THE AUTHOR

Fredrick Joseph Henley, Jr. earned a Doctor of Jurisprudence from Vanderbilt University and a Bachelor of Arts cum laude in English from Xavier University of Louisiana. Dr. Henley also holds the Project Management Professional (PMP) certification from the Project Management Institute. Most importantly, he is the husband of Vanessa and the father of two awesome daughters, Tayler & Christian. Prior to beginning his writing and speaking career, Dr. Henley served as a management consultant to Fortune 500 corporations & all levels of government. He also served as a University College instructor at Tulane University, practiced law and established a statewide ministry to incarcerated youth in Georgia.

ARTIST BIO

Obi Chidebelu-Eze was born in Enugu, Nigeria and came to the USA in 1989. He holds a Bachelor of Science degree from Oral Roberts University in Biology. He is employed as a scientist for Kimberly-Clark Corporation in Roswell, Georgia.

Obi has been honored to paint commissioned pieces, logos and jacket covers for books. In 2001, his first limited edition lithograph was released entitled 'Benin Chief Head'. And in 2002, his first color piece entitled 'Daughters Arise' was released. 'Daughters Arise' was created to accompany the book written by Dr. Fred Henley. Obi's art is constantly evolving. Like all art, he strongly believes that beauty is truly in the eye of the beholder.

NOTES

NOTES

NOTES

NOTES

NOTES

NOTES

NOTES

NOTES

NOTES

www.ingramcontent.com/pod-product-compliance
Lightning Source LLC
Chambersburg PA
CBHW032009040426
42448CB00006B/555